The National Poetry Series was established in 1978 to ensure the publication of five collections of poetry annually through five participating publishers. The Series is funded annually by Amazon Literary Partnership, William Geoffrey Beattie, the Gettinger Family Foundation, Bruce Gibney, HarperCollins Publishers, The Stephen and Tabitha King Foundation, Padma Lakshmi, Lannan Foundation, Newman's Own Foundation, Anna and Olafur Olafsson, Penguin Random House, the Poetry Foundation, Amy Tan and Louis DeMattei, Amor Towles, Elise and Steven Trulaske, and the National Poetry Series Board of Directors.

THE NATIONAL POETRY SERIES WINNERS
OF THE 2022 OPEN COMPETITION

Organs of Little Importance by Adrienne Chung
Chosen by Solmaz Sharif for Penguin Books

Tender Headed by Olatunde Osinaike
Chosen by Camille Rankine for Akashic Books

Survival Strategies by Tennison S. Black
Chosen by Adrienne Su for University of Georgia Press

I Love Information by Courtney Bush
Chosen by Brian Teare for Milkweed Editions

Sweet Movie by Alisha Dietzman
Chosen by Victoria Chang for Beacon Press

survival   strategies

survival

TENNISON S. BLACK

strategies

POEMS

THE UNIVERSITY OF
GEORGIA PRESS
ATHENS

Cover art by Coral Sue Black

Edna St. Vincent Millay, excerpt from "The courage that my mother had" from *Collected Poems*. Copyright 1954, © 1982 by Norma Millay Ellis. Reprinted with the permission of The Permissions Company, LLC on behalf of Holly Peppe, Literary Executor, The Millay Society, www.millay.org. "Harpers Ferry," from *Time's Power: Poems 1985–1988* by Adrienne Rich. Copyright © 1989 by Adrienne Rich. Used by permission of W. W. Norton & Company, Inc.

Published by the University of Georgia Press
Athens, Georgia 30602
www.ugapress.org
© 2023 by Tennison S. Black
All rights reserved
Designed by Kaelin Chappell Broaddus
Set in 10/13.5 Dolly Pro Regular by Kaelin Chappell Broaddus

Most University of Georgia Press titles are
available from popular e-book vendors.

Printed digitally

Library of Congress Control Number: 2023934363
ISBN: 9780820365152 (paperback)
ISBN: 9780820365169 (epub)
ISBN: 9780820365176 (PDF)

for the desert—I was wrong
and for Mama, he was, too

CONTENTS

after

FOREWORD

This is, simply, an important book. I'm so glad to have spent time with it. There is a somewhat mysterious word in Spanish, *querencia*, which loosely means belonging to or a longing for place. It is a word beyond logic, manifested in the human. These poems absolutely define that feeling, authenticating the vibrancy of longing, even while understanding that longing is a complex emotion.

These poems grow into a tour de force, a journey toward reckoning with the hard things in a hard place that make a life but do not always explain the why of it. In an absolute triumph of living over emotional drowning, the book centers itself with an extended prose poem, a deep dive that goes well beyond simply longing. It dives into the depths and shines a steady, small, and brave light. When the poems as separate entities connect enough, the floodgates of this book open and the multiple poems start to find themselves in one strong, absolute groundswell. This experience for the reader begins to read as if it were a flash flood.

The woman speaker is the same throughout so that we become confidantes in these tellings, establishing an intimacy that is often painful but also cathartic. We put the book down feeling like it is good for the author to have put these poems somewhere, to have given some kind of volume to an inside voice. As we read, we learn to do more than read—we learn to feel the moments, alive again. Whether this is fortunate or unfortunate is not the point—these moments, now, simply are. We, too, are witnesses.

The place in these poems is the West, in childhood, and from memory. But they do not trade on anything so grandiose as those words—we immediately start to live in Yuma, Arizona, toward the end of the last century. The world is a hot place, and tempers are even hotter.

All along, the reader is often given unaffected ways to measure that life and its people that aren't from a ruler or a spreadsheet. These measures often tell their own stories in a few words, making their measure consequential in a lived way. "Mama was a short woman with a steady eye, and in charge of everywhere she stood," for example, with a further later refinement on standing: "The bajada of a woman wore heels, not boots, and her hair added three inches to the top of her making her five-foot-seven at the bar and five-foot-four in the morning." That morning shows us more, something softer, which is hard to come by in this place: "she loved in cast-iron skillet gravy."

But the harder side of it all shows itself throughout: "There is a woman's paycheck in the creases of her forehead." Eventually, this woman takes her daughter and leaves: "Mama says she fled the culture—she means she fled the fists. / But it's the same." The daughter-speaker of these poems asserts throughout that "It's an eighty-seven-hour walk to Santa Ana // where lives Mama." We hear that measurement several times, a siren call to the Pacific and its ocean in place of desert. Much of these poems comes to terms with the idea that as rough as things seemed in the desert, it was perhaps more the roughness of those she was left with.

Cruelties come often and hard in these poems under the overwhelmingly deceptive guise of being regular life. Seen from the perspective of a child, without judgment, they are terrifying to the reader: "The cowboy and my mother, by turns, across / the state lines between them, put me in a slingshot, a plane, a / truck, and threw me at each other." This left the speaker in precarious situations: "A gun on your teeth / sounds like the grind of spur on gravel. No, it sounds like a // gun on teeth."

The veracity of this life shows up everywhere, not always in something so loud as a gun in the mouth, and indeed most persuasively in these poems' smallest moments. Sometimes the small moments come as voice, as words: "The / cowboy is six-foot-four with arms that wield chains or two- / buh-fours at rams and mules when they misbehave." Anyone who has been in this moment understands the colloquially regular "two-buh-fours." Sometimes the small things simply hold hands to make you ride a sentence as in this instance with the father: "The scent of Irish Spring and Old // Spice are gone. He's all beer and steer foam over horse lather / in the truck on the way home down two-lane roads / driving where he sees fit, right down the middle." In another instance, we get the small rejoinder, "My clothes crack when I take them off."

Cruelty, in its regular-life disguise, is sometimes difficult to sort. While there may be regular life in the moment that presents itself at first, life in these poems is invariably tinged with a sad and mean edge. "Rabbit, my favorite rabbit, hangs / by one foot in the tree, draining out, ready for stew." Sometimes the land itself is complicit—upon the speaker's return to the desert, "Creosote doesn't ask me where I've been, / but picks up like I wasn't gone." But in all of this, perhaps the most emotional to understand is the rock-hard simplicity of so many bottom lines. There is a kind of love in all this.

There is an element of didacticism in these poems, but it is most strongly aimed at the speaker herself, at her world and how she has grown to see it. It is the speaker speaking to herself at the far end of experience, the point at which one has some things to say, if now mostly, and most importantly, to herself. It begins, in one poem, as a question: "But the place I come from is ugly. Isn't it? No. // There are those who revere the desert. / So why can't I?" This is followed with a forceful answer in another poem: "I'll see silver tines, puncturevine, telson, stingers, barbs— / I'll love that beautiful answering hiss of the scorpions. / And the deal is, if I can see this, all of this, as beautiful, then / for once, I will see myself that way." It is a long road to this understanding.

The road is made harder, of course, by a lack of human clarity. The desert of this book is clear and hard, but the humans are simply hard, inexplicably so to the reader and, finally, to the speaker. "I was born in simultaneity— / here and on the other side of myself." To see the other side of things has taken a very long time.

Some answers lie, quite unfairly, in simply being a woman here, while at the same time this is what gives the speaker real courage and, finally, support: "Every seed of every woman has lived in the womb of every woman before her." Finally, let me say that these poems scare me, in the best ways possible. They provoke, dig, discover, argue, invent, all in ways I could not have done myself. In this way, they extend me.

They gift me with things beyond myself—feelings, glimmers, visions, understandings. Some of the poems will go far beyond this book, such as "Rodeo Night" and "The Mother and the Mountain," but all the pieces in this book, in tandem, simply give to us what was given to the speaker.

At one point, in a phrase that continues to haunt me, the speaker says: "I'm on my knees with remember."

ALBERTO RÍOS
Poet Laureate of Arizona,
Chancellor Emeritus of the
Academy of American Poets,
author of *Not Go Away Is My Name*

ACKNOWLEDGMENTS

My deepest thanks to the following for publishing some of these poems in earlier forms:

> *Bacopa Review* ("I Was Born for Rainy Days But")
> *Booth* ("The Confluence")
> *45th Parallel* ("Ten Is Too Girl")
> *Rough Cut Press* ("An Unquenchable Desire")
> *We Will Be Shelter* (anthology from Write Bloody Press;
>   "The Legacy of the Desert at Yuma")

The seeds of this book belong to a thousand growers. To Cynthia Hogue, admiration is too small a word; maybe awe is closer, but even then—just, thank you, for every seed a thank-you. And Norman Dubie, for the talks, the stones, the hours. To Alberto Ríos, Tito, for the courage and optimism. To Sally Ball for the incredible insight and talks, for teaching me how to teach. To the Virginia G. Piper writer's center and the research grant, which gave me room to finish. To Kamea, with her sharp insight and incredible force of will, you are forever my first true love, my best reader. To Coral and her immeasurable loving loyal support, for the belief that this was in me—and for the talks—you are my buoy, my PFD. To Solstice, for being the magic, always, for all of the things you remind me to believe in, including myself—for being my biggest fan. For Mama, in all ways and all things, all my love.

Special thanks to Adrienne Su for selecting *Survival Strategies* for the National Poetry Series. And also to the readers, organizers, and entire team of the NPS—I stand in awe of what you do.

And finally, tremendous gratitude and bottomless thanks to the team at UGA including Beth, Elizabeth, Jon, Kaelin, and so many more—my thanks over and over for your care and attention. How lucky and amazing to get to work with you all.

survival strategies

the sunniest place on earth

We are woman and nature.
And he says he cannot hear us speak.
But we hear.
—SUSAN GRIFFIN

We realize that the liberation of all oppressed peoples necessitates
the destruction of the political-economic systems of capitalism and
imperialism as well as patriarchy.
—COMBAHEE RIVER COLLECTIVE

I Was Born for Rainy Days But

I was born in the Sonoran.
And I keep thinking

> *She's missing me, if a desert can miss—*
> *it does miss me, it has to.*

Meaning I need it to because what am I otherwise?
If everything I leave or that has left me doesn't miss me, then
over here at invisible o'clock I still want to feel

comfortable being called a visible Woman,
being called by a name, being seen
but I don't.

I'm the thing who can't forget that Arizona
has been trying to kill me since I was born into it. But even
if it hates me, I still get these urges for the touch

of the dirt I left in a huff some forty-odd years ago.
And suddenly I'm all *please take me back*
I'm sorry   I WON'T DO IT AGAIN   *You're beautiful, Ay-Zee.*

Like my first husband.
But I don't really mean it, like my third.
Because I'm holding a grudge.

Because I never thought it was beautiful in the Sonoran
until I'd been away for decades
until I grew up and got away enough to look

backward at it. Like the way I look at
pictures of my twenties and remember how
gross I felt, how awkward, all angles and elbows,

stick-out ribs and buck teeth—how unwanted—but now
I realize I was always lovely in the soft skin of youth.
And I'm sad for young me for whom the word Woman

was a wound infected with the cowboy gaze.
When I left, I told the scrub, the sand and scorpions, saguaro
and especially the cowboys—I told everyone

except the painted ponies, the birds, the jackrabbits,
everyone but the red-threaded iron-rich rocks and the women
who held my hands whenever they found me lost—which

was often—I told all of the rest of it except that which is too
precious to let go of that they were unwanted, and
I threw hate at them in darts and daggers.

I hated *at* all of it—the sounds and smells, the scratchy
way of living I was born into. I waved up an exorcism of
my origin, of the destructive, violent invasion of cowboy

culture. But I'm going back, anyway. Because
I left something of me in the desert.
Because you can't imagine the glory of a jackrabbit

on the run at full-tilt fleeing the dusk-fired coyote
across a dirt road until you've seen it, and you can't
know yourself until you know who you're rooting for.

An Unquenchable Desire

Sonoran kids wear the kind of dirt that hasn't seen rain
or dew since winter last,

and even then the gathering of wet
was three-hundredths of an inch.

My clothes crack when I take them off.
The dirt of the desert breaks under boots

in a way that's more snap than grind,
where steps go on top but moisture hides.

The water flees the dirt, afraid of the way the sun sits
too close. Afraid of what the sun does to moisture,

the way the sun sits hip to hip
with the dirt. Water is afraid of the sun's

whisker burn, an old man too close and leaning in,
breathing out stale billows of beer and cigarillos.

Water longs to learn a love for heat by way of missing it.
Fondness via absence.

When I said I wished for rain, Mama answered,
Wishing never made rain when the rain was afraid to fall.

Here I Am

In the sage, blowing smoke, the creosote's whisper
won't ask where I've been, won't have missed me.
But I'm older now—and don't care.
Not because I really don't care.

But because care is more than I can do
in this body, right now.
Which place misses a person, anyway?
We are the sad who go looking for happy

instead of growing it. We are the loneliness of air
before it's breathed. The want to be absorbed
into something. To dissolve.
Be absolved.

Creosote doesn't ask me where I've been
but picks up like I wasn't gone,
says, *Javelina's been at my roots, again.*
Deserts don't miss people when they leave.

The Legacy of the Desert at Yuma

The Sonoran is a place where staying alert means staying
alive. The jumpy Gila monster is a barn-found saw blade
hidden under a pillow and one of only a few venomous
lizards in the world. Coyote calls you to distraction and

hails the peccary on the night spiked frigid—that breeder
of shivers chasing after an escaping sun. Hollers from the
hands bring the heelers to work. This is where the theft
of a river saved the colonizers,

delivered a living under rifle watch. And hence the mighty
Colorado, moving south, became little more than a creek.

Something to Hold On To

I've inherited the fallacy of a universal benevolence.
I want the desert to care that I'm back.

I search for kestrel, looking for some connection.
Trying to prove we're in the same nest. *Remember me.*

Please. Remember me. I was born
into a pecan grove in the Sonoran. By the old barracks

of the workers, the longhouse now derelict clapboard in
the light of a red after-storm's dusk. But the picker's nest

is empty. They've all been tossed or turned out. The trees are
a nuisance of droppings now. Steam weaves through

the branches, catches my lens and fogs the glass. What's
gone is gone and blows across the desert as bush bones; I

guess people call them tumbleweeds. But we kids didn't. In
the picker's kitchen of 1977 it smells like ranch beans and

ham hocks. *Girl, get to work, what you doing chasing them?*
You gonna curl your fingers around the tail of a mustang?

The Sunniest Place on Earth

Land of the Quechan, the Kwatsáan;
Kokwapa, of Cocopah   utterly plundered.

Home to the YTP, where colonizers landed in the driest place,
built a river pass and called it a migrant's crossing,

like anyone was allowed to do so. Turned the mighty
Colorado into a ditch and added a fort. Called the place

a gateway, like it made people want more. 1886–1900 cotton
habits pace on the porch of a prison, but they call it a school.

Genocide labeled language acquisition. And the white
history books call them heroes. 1875–1909 at the other prison,

29 women and 3,040 men kept in a hole in the Sonoran. Now
they call it an attraction with photos and a walking tour. They

put the high school there a year after it closed in 1909. Seems
apropos but now Criminals are a logo and merch

comes from the Cell Block. Yes, really. The merch store is
called the Cell Block in the sunniest place on Earth.

The Confluence

This is the bullseye of the sun. At the narrowest point, a natural crossing place of the Colorado River where the banks were, back then, less than one thousand feet across. Thus they built a ferry crossing so people, no, not all people, but some people—we all know which people—could get to and from California. Colonials sat down crisscross and armed at the confluence of the two rivers: the Gila and the Colorado, sure, but also of Fort Yuma and the Cocopah, of smoke and water, of heat and cicada, of Arizona, California, and Mexico. And they violenced a Western colonial town out of the valley of smoke where there wasn't empty nothing. It wasn't empty nothing. They built a siphon into the river. It pays to be upstream. Built a prison, built a "school," which is redundant, and the cowboys and politicians held up their greed to the sun; lines over lines, they obscured the footprints that were already there with their jackboots. The smoke valley with her smoke from hearth fires, dwelling fires, cooking fires, drying fires, rain-call fires of families, of the Cocopah, Kokwapa, and Quechan, Kwatsáan in their homes. And the colonials told *them* they had to pay *six hundred dollars* in property taxes. River's valley ransacked as an afterthought of how to cross the Colorado and get to the gold in California. This is the sunniest place *in the world*, the fifth-driest dot on the marble. Not towel dry, or ash dry— air-of-casket dry, cracked-open-petrified-bone dry, crumbling- skin dry, three millimeters of rain in a *year*, diatomaceous place, dried-up ocean, salted valley can't cry, but it's made of tears, driest place in all of the states, dry. Have you ever tried to take a bite of cricket flour and silica from a spoon? Now swallow it. An encyclopedia entry for the end of days with the King of Arizona presiding. And there, two rivers converged and made love to keep The People alive. The Gila, and the Colorado. *There. Right there.*

Grab it, that spot, build a river pass. Let's call it a migrant's crossing, a welcome from the people just arrived to those already there, bullshit over bravado. Wave the cowboy hats in the air. Say hello. Turn a river into an American dream using a siphon. Turn a river into a ditch. A ditch, a military fort. *It's a Gateway. Okay?* A way to welcome some—but don't ever forget it's never all—to the proving ground. Proven ground of the river's two thousand years of inhabitants. The autochthonous made into the unwelcome. The Colorado was the savior of the colonials. It delivered life to the driest land they'd ever stolen.

The Crime Might Just Be the Law

for No Más Muertes

I'm an instigator who nudges rules
to suit myself. Not the big ones but
what is an OUT door if not the path
of the easiest entrance?
Can't imagine where that came from,

but you'd know if you ever met
my mother. I tilt the world toward thank
you, now *let me go.*
Every day of my life I've stood,
arms thrown wide on the back

of a moving truck. Charging
through the glare, trying to catch
the sun so I could find the moon.
At some point I came to believe
in water. That the water that cut

the Grand Canyon went somewhere
when it was finished and if I looked
hard enough, I could find it.
Of course, I also believed
for a few minutes

just before I turned seventeen
that the world's problems were caused
by meanness. Because I'd never heard
of cruelty.
But that was when I didn't know people

kill for fun and sport. And what is growing
up anyway, except for learning that there are
those who believe with stubborn ferocity
that *leaving water in the desert* should be
a felony (read that again) despite it

being not just our right, but our obligation,
no, not just our obligation, but the proof
of our humanity? Or the lack thereof.

The Dare

I make deals with myself
that I won't cry or hurt or burn with sadness
when I stand in the eye of the desert again and look
down on myself from the dunes, watching my skin burn.

The deliberate nature of my choice to go back is the difference
between hate and whole. Sand-trapped and dunesledding.
This time I will carefully look on the beauty—
yes, of sharp things and dry things, scratchy and hard things.

I'll see silver tines, puncturevine, telson, stingers, barbs—
I'll love that beautiful answering hiss of the scorpions.
And the deal is, if I can see this, all of this, as beautiful, then
for once, I will see myself that way.

The Meaning of Salt

When I let chuckwalla crawl across these dirty old feet
now covered in scars and dry patches—

when I taste the Sonoran's sun on my bare skin, hear my boots
in the dirt, in the dark, part crack

crunch   part grind of rock   parted salty lips
maybe I'll hear my mother. Taste what salt means.

And then I will see what I am made of.
And I won't feel utterly lost

anymore. Because I was born *there*.
As if birthplace isn't random.

As if it's not all happenstance and luck.
But the place I come from is ugly. Isn't it? *No.*

There are those who revere the desert.
So why can't I?

estivate so you don't die

Not Ready to Make Nice
—THE CHICKS

If you are silent about your pain,
they'll kill you and say you enjoyed it.
—ZORA NEALE HURSTON

One Wooden Girl

The girl, seven, reached out of a car window, leaned for love of a heeler: blue, the color of creek shadow. Spotted and made of pure muscle, this dog was her friend while she was at the ranch. She stuck that hand out of the window because the dog was one of the few joys she found in this place. She reached for fur, said the dog's name, Stoker, stretched away from the sweltering lonely in the car made more so by the desert and melted thighs on vinyl seats—and a stepbrother who rode shotgun until made to ride in back with a hated *girl*. It was hot. And leaning out of the window offered some relief. The front seat had a striped madras seat cover. But I'm only saying that as a distraction because I don't want to own what happened. The old cruiser, bought at surplus, painted budget green on a Los Algodones side street, scattered gravel turning into the ranch while the dog ran toward my stick-out hand, waving in the wind out of the window, a wooden oar of girl, and as the dog ran toward me—the car bumped over Stoker's body. And my stepbrother informed me in a low tone, as if recapping the latest episode of *Gunsmoke*, that he was going to kill me.

Idyll of the Liars' Rain

Prickers covered her socks. She left them until they wore off
because picking hurt her small fingers. In the predawn, three
quiet faces, one old enough for coffee, sat silent on the springy

truck bench on the way to the edge of town. She rode in the
middle between a cowboy and scorpion/stepbrother because
middles are for girls, girls who aren't anything like the boys

they find themselves between. This girl was made of a throw-
away woman, a second wife. The Palo Verde woods come up
before crusty dusted headlights, whispering with creosote in

the copse at a Yuma ranch at dawn. The trees rub each other,
rattle, laugh like a crinkly skirt, hanging, turning in the air.
A woman sits crisscross applesauce in the trees. Deep

seconds pass, and she turns slowly as they pull up, looks
at the matted girl. Right at her. A yellow flannel blanket with
tender blue satin edging wraps a doll in the girl's lap, and they

alight with a landing more thud than grace, more plunk than
stand, more prickers. Beside the woman, a moderate horse,
a creamed-coffee and ochre-spotted appaloosa. Reins drag the

ground, conchos ajangle, dancing *ching ching* in the dither
of the mare, soft as a shrill whisper. Atop the laden mare's
back, a woven blanket in red, black, and cream chevroned

diamonds cushion her from a spindly cage. A wooden top
holds in place bleached bone bars ajut at every angle. Inside,
stacked and shuffling, edging for space, wings to breasts,

beaks nosing up, two dozen or more gray and tan doves singing
coo-coo-caloo. Mare and woman linger. Lived-in
hands pet the velvet muzzle. The mare flows urine into the

sand and creosote, now wetted, wakes and ruffles the air
with the scent of a liar's rain. The woman admonishes the
mare and tousles her head. She breathes steam despite the

warming air, stands, ticks her fingertips along the cage spires
and pickets. The ticking reaches the girl, and she stares. The
cowboy loads his guns and lays them one next to the other in a

row on a splintered log at his feet. Sound comes from every
direction—a whoop, caw, cry, yell, slap, sting, yup, bark, and
birds are flushed from everywhere, wings like tossing time in

hot oil. Guns flash, pop, blast, crack, whip, roar, wham, the
morning is broken open—her tiny hands on the girl's ears are
gnats. A pittance. The woman sits in the stand of trees, criss-

cross applesauce, beside the mare. The gesture from the cowboy
is
rough, a thrown point—a yell over warfare—and
the scorpion thrusts out toward the trees, picks up a fallen bird

on the way, circles, sweeps around and comes back, dropping
a pile behind the cowboy. One is missed, half-alive, and laying
halfway between the woman and girl who won't look away

from the mare, floundering as she is over the boundary
between there and here. The boy swoops out again. Grabs the
flopping life. Life is noise. Life is twisting in the sand, hurt,

bleeding. Life shouldn't lay in the prickers. The baby doll
lands in the dirt. Life is wrapped in yellow flannel with tender

blue edging. Life has gray feathers and little eyes. There is love in looking. The mare paces, draws infinity in the sand with her reins. The woman sits inside infinity. The pile of no-more-life grows over three hours while life breathes, coos,

and looks. The girl looks too, rocks life back and forth. Pets the soft head. *What—is this?* spake the cowboy. *She wrapped one of the dead doves in her stupid baby blanket—I told her*

not to, spake the scorpion. But it wasn't dead. Not yet. Life fell away when the blanket was snatched. Life moved. Life was in the prickers. The cowboy grabbed life by the neck and

shook it roughly once, then dropped no-more-life on the pile. The woman stood, looked toward the girl, caught the reins, and walked with the mare through the trees and out into the

sand. The *ching, ching* of dancing conchos fading. The sun caught her coat. It was made of feathers. An empty cage sat open on the mare's back.

Like a Dead Dove's a Doll

The sun falls down the mesa stairs
chasing after its own horizon,
fleeing the heat of the day.

Hollers from working hands bring the blue
heelers to work at dawn, so better get going on the night.
We don't waste the dark around here.

Dusk draws wives toward the stove.
A late-60s bouncing dip-brown F-250 races down the drive
coming in from the field with a spray of kicked-up dust,

scattering gravel and cowboys into the little home's yard.
Rowdies spill from the truck bed,
toss a hog into the pit,

two hands at each end, swinging dead pig
like it's a child's game: 1, 2, *swing out, back*,
when the day ends in dinner to feed forty,

when the picking's done and the alfalfa comes in,
mesquite smoke and steam rise up from red coals lined with
wet burlap and the waft of burning hair,

the singe of hogskin makes the beer taste better.
The night rolls in thick, spikes frigid goose bumps
on drying salted skin, leaves damp chills on the neck,

raising shivers after the day's sweat.
Sweat here gathers on the skin just for standing,
am'ing, be'ing, staying put. Never mind working.

It's 112° at 4:00 but by 9:00 when they dig up the hog
it takes whiskey to keep warm.
I hear the hands talking.

They say I didn't earn my sweat. *She don't work*
much, is pretty useless all around. Well, mostly.
She's okay for lookin' at. Tell her to do something though,

an' she's as likely to spend the task daydreaming as doing it.
My father joins in to help elaborate, *Tell her to run out and*
go fetch a downed dove from the field while you reload.

The next thing you know she's
wrapping that twitchy dying bird in that damned
blue dolly blanket, like a dead dove's a doll.

Slaughter a rabbit for dinner, a rabbit you raised, mind,
a rabbit you spent good money bringing up
for that very purpose and she'll cry all damned night

like you didn't try to feed her.
No matter what, she'll spend half a week refusing to eat.
Like most girls, she's not worth much.

My father spits into the dirt on his way to the cooler.
She's okay for lookin' at, says another,
and winks at me. *But she's lazy as a Cadillac's bumper.*

He Wonders Why I Never Call

Birthed in Yuma by the daughter of a dairy farmer
who turned pecan picker for love when she
fell prey to the charms of a North Dakota cowboy,
I was born in simultaneity—
here and on the other side of myself.

If you flip me around, you'll see
I'm the same on both sides.
The morning after my birth
they placed me,
the violin in its case,

under the open window of their shack,
notes of dust and desert a hum in the screenless hole.
They were unprepared, my parents,
not because they didn't expect or want me
but because I lived when several before me had been lost

in pregnancy, delivery, or shortly after birth.
I was early, and tumbleweed isn't nesting material.
Mama called me shithead.
Kestrel called me a sound over the din,
a sound like the beat before the crack of a pebble on glass.

The hung air that breaks the noise open. Imagine a child
always chasing silence.
Scorpion called me stupid. *I'll say it to her face.*
The cowboy called me *a girl.* Which sounded
like he'd never like me anyhow.

The Last Photograph

There remains one photograph, a pink-tinted picture of
the three of us, its edges soft and warped, framed by pecan
branches. The pecans and I were born in Yuma, shadescaped
into believing we belonged, though each was made
for somewhere else.

I'm maybe two, astride a velvet-brown horse. The cowboy
is there wearing pride. And Mama with forehead creases
worried about her baby on this horse. The cowboy's chest is
puffed out in a shield of hubris. He's just bought that horse
after he won the cockfight, came home

and drug us into the yard, put me up top. Mama is a perfect
doll in lipstick and a pencil skirt. Her lips in a bow. The
cowboy is six-foot-four with arms that wield chains or two-
buh-fours at rams and mules when they misbehave.
Mules are bred from a horse and a donkey. They are sterile.

And some say stubborn. And cowboys—at least this cowboy
isn't known for being patient with rebellion. When mules
rebel, there is a chain or a board, or a post, nearby—or a fist,
a rope. Maybe a tire iron. And his arms
are a muscle memory of every time

someone on this arm has rebelled against the cowboy's will.
The horse is squared off side-eye to the camera, veins running
ribbons down his legs, the earned thoroughbred pose from
California, the last in his line. He's valuable.
I'm on the horse, unnamed still in my own head. But the horse

is *Concho* it says on the back of the fading pink picture. Between
my parents, I'm in a lopsided boat. Tipping
into the deep end of divorce. The cowboy is tall and sturdy
and Mama small and elegant. I'm neither. Concho eyes the
pecan tree like he can't remember how he got there. My 2T

legs and stick-out feet on the saddle, stirrups hanging lonely,
swinging. I have no memory of this moment
or what it felt like for us to be together
except in this one image that rewrites any memory
to the tune of a never-sung song.

Mama says she fled the culture—she means she fled the fists.
But it's the same. We ran toward the hush of the ocean and
settled with one suitcase and each other. The cowboy told me
when last we spoke, I'm still just like my mother.
Whom he calls a mule. A beautiful mule.

Nameskins

Mama would try a name on me,
pull it on over my once-downy head
and out over the coarse limbs of her raggedy girl,

something alliterative—Stephanie Susan, Maggie Marie.
The cowboy and Mama were clever.
And *the little shit* that I was

wouldn't answer when called.
I chafed at the concept of naming—nothing suited.
Nothing felt comfortable. Every name was binding. *Names by*

the damned, naming namers all, I said to the rabbits.
And they told me, *You were born a weed, Girl.*
Why do you care what they call you?

In the course of as many years, I wore eight names,
most I chose myself and quickly outgrew—
something fantastic—Lorelei, Titania,

Emily, Suzy, Carin, Charlotte.
I hung these up like patterned jumpsuits,
shed nameskins,

took them off,
put another on,
hooked them on cactus tines,

left them to dry in the sun—until
they crumpled with the dry, sonorous *shhhhhh*
of the Sonoran—noiseless if you weren't a careful listener

and no one was,
so a girl, a *little shit*, in her blue dress
blew away in ashes.

Ivy over a Crumbling Facade

I would chase name bits around cattishly,
pretend I'd wear them again, flaunt them

like long ladies' gloves,
lick them from my fingers when I was finished with each

while mama told me how pretty they were on me,
how they fit me just right. Practically begging me

to keep one, any one.
The cowboy said they made me look, sound,

seem, better than I really was—
and what an endowment.

Making tea from dandelions. Deliciousness from twigs.
Names such as can ivy one's architecture, cover the

broken parts—abet the glossing of my identity.
Not one of these names since I took them off

have been as pretty to me as they once were.
Upon later meeting a Suzy, Destiny, Lorelei,

I would remember the feeling
of wearing their names and, for that day, feel shame.

Each time I felt that I'd ensorcelled them somehow.
Sullied that which was perfectly good on someone else.

And I've yet to find one that wasn't worse off
for having been worn by me and discussed by them.

I Divorced the Desert

The cowboy and my mother, by turns, across
the state lines between them, put me in a slingshot, a plane, a
truck, and threw me at each other. Take two people who
never could get along and put a child between them,
I'm sure they'll work it out.

I rode the yellow line between them a few times every year,
sat in the road on stops, looked up at semitrucks, told
the air horns and asphalt, the roadside flowers and
crumpled barns long stories of the ocean I missed when she
sent me back to Yuma, to his side of the line. I knew the desert

and the ocean hadn't seen one another in a very long
time—I was a sort of emissary then. I called to the ocean
through the open window as we turned toward Yuma and any
kestrel that might hear me, hoping they'd respond when I sang
killi killi killi killi killi.

The roadrunner, the javelina, the lizards all tell stories of the
ocean that was once theirs and I want to be a listening person.
But I hated this desert. The volley of my life between the
ocean and the sage. I began to hate the drifts of sand at the
edges of everything, the scrub that scratched and burned

tender skin. Every summer, every spring break, every
other Xmas. This way over the net, now back, and again. My
suitcase stuffed with resentment.
I was made of pigtails and pillowcase dresses with spades
for scapulas. And growing fast. In one day I went from Leia buns

to skinny jeans. But for a while I brinked between
girl and indignant. More girl, less indignant, then reversed, a
teeter-totter back and forth by miles. I only laughed when
I was at the ocean.
And I rarely spoke when I wasn't.

In case you wondered, it's an eighty-seven-hour walk
from Yuma to Santa Ana.
But I never made it past four and with eighty-three to go
I always turned back
before they ever went looking.

Survival Strategies I

When the rains don't come—and they won't
because Yuma is the sunniest place on Earth,
which sounds great in the abstract. Like
a sunburned Anaheim theme park, but
Ocotillo shed their leaves to preserve energy.

Spadefoot toads estivate so they don't die—
that is, they sleep for nine months of the year. Little girls
who like animals more than people narrate the silica,
carve stories onto their skin with cactus tines, but also
shade beetles with cupped hands while they cross roadways

and fall in love with rabbits to stay alive. Kangaroo
rats never need drink a drop. They receive all they will
ever need from eating leaves. To conserve energy
roadrunners run in lieu of flight. Bobcats hunt
dust devils for practice, to keep sharp

when food is scarce. River toads have a patch
on their bellies which will rehydrate them as they sit
in or on tiny gatherings of moisture because Yuma
receives just 85 millimeters of rain per year. Less than three paper
clips long. Little girls talk to cholla.

Are you lonely
because no one
loves you?
Ask kestrel, *Will you fly me to my mama?*
And cry an ocean from missing one.

Mamas, Don't Make Your Daughters with Cowboys

Buckets of green-brown water
get tossed on the creosote by cowboys
with shirtsleeves in a Skoal-roll just for the smell.

Tin buckets drawn dripping from horse troughs make
tosswater for the smell of a liar's rain.
The scent of desert rain comes from the creosote's

lying leaves. It's not rain, but it sure smells like it —
Rain won't come here,
won't because it's too dry to waste itself.

Why throw down on scrub
in a three-minute evaporation?
It won't come because its run off north

looking for a better reception than cowboys.
Cowboys pace at the scent of pork in the pit with
yellow Coors cans in the hand that in't tossing horseshoes.

Someone's fucking against the backside of the barn.
Smoke and a liar's rain. Garlic and singed hog hair.
At the hog pit, skeeters hump blood from sun-worn bodies,

ripped bodies, strap stout and spattered with old-timer scars.
Skin stretched thin over muscle made from sheep shearing and
baling hay, arms made for the rodeo ring. Arms

made for hunting, for butchering,
arms that wrangle,
arms that toss their little girls like dead pigs—

but in the air, not in the pit.
Catch them once a year
by the braids and slap them for telling a boy no.

Arms that point and tell little girls to fetch
yellow cans from the cooler with a pat
on the backside. *G'awn now, scoot.*

Tell them they look pretty
and ignore their struggle
like the rest of the livestock.

Rodeo Night

*When I am at rodeo I find it difficult not to root for
the animals.*
—DEMETRI MARTIN

In Yuma, it's rodeo night. And dinner comes late on rodeo
night. *Cows ain't pets, girl.* The hands chase me out of the
pens. *Get lost. Unless ya wanna—tonguetonguetonguetongue
they waggle at me.* Eyebrows, among other things.

It's two o'clock, and it smells like Coors in red cups,
summer sausage breath, and the reek of ranch hands
turned out to prowl for a night getting too close.
You wanna play a game? They demand kisses

for luck. Take them if I don't acquiesce. Sudden tongue in
my mouth. *Whoops,* they laugh. The four o'clock breeze hits
briefly, carrying the waft of hotdogs, warm ketchup, dip spit
on leather, saddle soap. By eight the air coming in

from the desert tastes of alfalfa wet with evening
irrigation from algae-slick ditches, manure, and sweat
on salt-chapped lips. Girls don't always scream.
Here comes the night. Rodeo night tastes like cussing,

shit, for the first time when you can't be heard, like the way
salt makes watermelon sweeter. I want to wrap my tender
feet in steel-toed boots. I want to feel safe. But I wear Thrifty
Drug flip-flops with holes in the soles. Under the stands

at the rodeo, under the people, I've walked away from
mewling calves caught by ropes—can't stand their
cries. Or the cows bleating for their babies, teats overfull.
There I'm hidden from hoots and catcalls, the thrown rocks

of the boys. I climb under, then peer
out through the gaps of the bleacher pipes at the daggered eyes
of a steer. It glowers through the cracks in a culture that two
species make when they gaze into each other

from the edges. We stare. A kestrel cries
overhead. I lick my fingers, then the trail of watermelon juice
from near my elbow to my wrist. The steer huffs, paws the
crusty dirt in his pen. *I ain't afraid of you. Where's your*

mother? He wants to feel safe. The crackle of the prod makes
him look away, swish his tail, turn toward the sound. As the
current connects with his anus, he bolts toward the gate. Drafted.
He's six hundred pounds of muscle and horns in a game made

by men who wear belts made of the slaughter and wrangle.
Buckles of silver pride. A kestrel's striped feather lays on
the ground in the fluff of bleacher dust. I stick the feather in
my hair. The plume juts out awkwardly from the Leia buns

I made of the braids I was given. I chase stray cats from
lickable candy wrappers, suck melted chocolate from
remainders, chew sandy popcorn, hunt for Red Vine dropsies and
pocket treasures, ground scores of old lighters, coins, and lonely

earrings. All of these land in the Holly Hobbie pockets
of my pillowcase dress with rickrack edging and fuzzy red
yarn straps beside stones I've sucked until they are wet and
colorful. Through the gaps in the lowest bleacher treads, I can

see the rodeo ring. The cowboy chases the steer
from his saddle, pulls the horse this way and that, leans out
with a hand on the saddle horn. He's far from center, but
the horse bears his weight, pounds the face of the sand,

throwing stress. The steer veers, thundering toward the edges
of the ring; foam lathers his lips. They all—the horse, the cowboy,
and the steer—reek of fear. The cowboy, bulldogger, is 6'4" tall and
240 pounds. He looks sharp. A rancher should on rodeo night,

hanging as he does in the breadth
of air when he has thrown himself from the running horse
and toward the fleeing steer. Caught in photographs forever
in midair, legs one way and arms the other. American cowboy,

leaping, suspended, defiant. The bull, the horse, gravity—
everything belongs to him. The hat is either on, the model
of cowboy willpower, or a flying blur, an examination
of the way that even cowboys are subject to the forces

of nature. Viewers will admire his humanity in this moment.
But the cowboy's head without his hat is a lie.
The steer, wrenched by his horn, with one angling toward
the dirt and the bulk of him forcibly twisted toward the fall,

howls. Above his dress-Wranglers, which are held on by his
best tooled belt, with his name on the back and his brass and
silver buckle from his last win, the cowboy wears his best
hat and a clean shirt with pearlized snaps, hand-set by his new

wife with a setting pin, a tiny hammer, and a steel bar. The
pockets and cuffs are edged in navy blue piping and, in the
seam, three drops of her blood to keep him safe. This
is a thing my mama never did for him. She was

a woman who didn't use her magic on men. The shirt wasn't
among the fanciest there that night, but it was clean and
pressed, starched. The plaid of it marked this cowboy as
a little bit old-timey. The kind of man who admires John

Wayne over Clint Eastwood and eventually Clint Eastwood
over Bruce Willis. The kind of man who
insists that *it's just a joke*, while telling you in the next breath
how many Black people work for him or are his friends.

The steer bellows, squalls *No. No*, in vibrato, he's a tenor; he
yowls hell into the hum of the stands, addresses his horn to the
cowboy. *No, you there*. Maybe hopes for spatchcock when
the hip of the bulldogger comes down on his side,

misses the horn, hip to neck, and ranch-made hands
grab his horns, wrench his head to the side. The horse
has gone on to wait by the gate. A witness. There are a thousand
popping flashbulbs as the flail of dirt clears. The cowboy walks

toward the horse. I see myself
in the bull, the horse, not the cowboy—who's proven something,
he thinks. The fans all think about his prowess. People yell, cheer,
hooray the cowboy. Beer splashes down from above,

into my hair. The sign flashes his time. He doesn't look.
Cowboy confidence is his primary objective. Instead, he
winks at his wife and a few others. She's watching the
clock so he doesn't have to. The scent of Irish Spring and Old

Spice are gone. He's all beer and steer foam over horse lather
in the truck on the way home down two-lane roads
driving where he sees fit, right down the middle. A new
belt buckle rests in a box on the seat. He beat his best time.

He's grinning at me bouncing along on the madras seat cover
in the middle of the bench seat, but I won't look at him
and instead watch the window, tracing the ditches with
my eyes, imagining dolphins, moths, mercy. I'm dusted

such that my eyelashes are gray. Streaks of skin peek
through dirt in sweat trails that hide my freckles. The
driveway cuts around the field and scatters into the yard before
the barn. Sheep and grapefruit trees make specters

in the twilight. Rabbit, my favorite rabbit, hangs
by one foot in the tree, draining out, ready for stew. I start to cry
but he taps his belt and looks at me.
Dinner comes late on rodeo night.

Ten Is Too Girl

ten is too girl to know
his finger is on the detonator of my life

a field of burrs in sand
i vomit him. bubbles of heat pop on my skin

blisters that prick, tick   tock
wait wait. everything is wait.

until the phone rings and i
hope it's my mother. *i want to come home.*

scuffed jellies aren't desert footwear
but there's School House Rock punctuation in my head

and the cowboy never bought me anything. no, not once.
the blue dog, the one they call a bitch,   digs

under desert scrub for shade. drinks
limeade not water because ten is too girl

to want water when there's limeade and i share.
i'm hesitant to merge with what's next? wait. wait. now.

i'm the first in line after the ambulance
all rush and no thought, trying to get away

from being stuck. struck.
it's Saturday morning and

I'm trying to wake   up
make some fucking

coffee.
bring me a beer   a bitch

is how it smells when he wakes up.
two months in the summer and every other

Christmas—one foot hovering over the date
the wait

trampled under the rodeo hooves
wicked girl wrong girl too ~~girl~~ bitch

just like her mother
i got lost in sight of the Hollywood sign

was wearing something, it doesn't matter what
i was. no, *you're really something*, but it doesn't sound like

something good. chin dripping and laughing when
i'm not there gulping limeade to not die

ten is too girl to smell like the men who have
already touched me   to be a bitch

or anything other than a girl
drinking limeade.

When Your Father Is a Cowboy

A man deserves a second chance,
but keep an eye on him.
—JOHN WAYNE

When Mama called to check on me,
my stepmother said, *She's out with the rabbits, playing.*
But the lid of the cedar chest cracked

when the cowboy sat down, pulling off his belt
through old jeans—rodeo buckle end in huge hands,
his name in the middle of the tooled leather.

Four letters, with room for the belt loop in the middle.
He said, *How old are you now?* And I guess he didn't know,
so I held up fingers just over a handful.

One for each year, he said, and I tried to run
but fast hands, from catching pigs, lashed out, and my ponytail
trailed behind, so I never stood a chance, and he bent me

over his lap and pulled down my pants.
One hand exposed me to the belt and the other swung.
For every sound, he said, he'd *add one.*

When it was over, the rabbit hutches were me-sized caves
with furry neighbors for fingers needing the comforting
touch of something alive,

something soft, soothing.
My stepmother added, *Oh yeah, she's happy as can be.*
But can't come to the phone right now.

Survival II

Damnable beast they call javelina, arguing with the Gila
monster, pissed at the rattlesnake, commotion
in the creosote, shaker shaker of leaves and a rugged
obstinance of power. Chitter chitter the tusks that rub, fillet.

We don't live here because we have to. We live here
because we scried the clouds and saw that here
we outlive you. Roadrunner are one of the few who call
the rattlesnake prey. They can do so because they're whip-quick

as they taunt the rattler, daring it to strike, and then as it does,
they step aside, catching the snake by the head to avoid
the deadly bite. Finally, they smash the snake's head on the
ground over and over, for up to fifteen minutes, until death

dims the fight. River toads are toxic enough to kill large dogs,
but raccoons pull them from the water by a hind leg and eat
them belly first to avoid the poison. Chuckwalla crawl inside
tight spaces, then inflate their bodies with air to fill the space

and make it difficult for predators to dislodge them. When the
ram broke my tibia, the cowboy told me I was *being a girl* and
instructed me to *walk it off. Being tough is the only way.* I
thought he was cruel, still do, though I also now see

there is wisdom in learning to manage the pain of existence
by any of these means. Be quick. Choose carefully before
eating. Let nothing disturb your rest. And be strong when you
can. But there is also this: if every memory your child has of

you is one of cruelty or mean-spiritedness, you are likely to die
lonesome in a home having not seen her in many many years.

Keep Your Eyes on the Monsters

Saguaro have fellowship in little girls
who are too prickly for friends, or who
can't find any. Cactus grow and girls
tell them stories, make sculptures from pricker
burrs—three atop each other,

conversant toys who sing "Rainbow Connection"
with spike noses, thorn legs,
hats of ocotillo-speared leaves, and stink-bug shoes.
Creosote coaches us to save the best of ourselves
for the rain.

Ants swarm my feet. I swipe, wipe, stamp.
The bites burn red. Scorpion-boy goes to get the gasoline
and a match. I crawl under the mesquite for shade.
Prickle skin bristles against my shoulder;
tusks draw arrows in the air.

Stop. The wire hairs of the javelina
stand on end. I puff my cheeks in hello.
They scuff feet and hooves,
meet my eyes.
It's a face-off. The scent of dinner rides in

on the mosquitoes over the musk.
A truck passes on the road.
We settle in. Neither moves. Inertia
builds, rolls in waves into the low spots. My eyes droop.
I lay my cheek in the dirt beside the resting animal.

A horse dithers at the scrub outside, reins dragging.
Cicadas lather the air with *currha, currha, currha.*
It's an eighty-seven-hour walk from Yuma to Santa Ana.
Javelina puffs a breathy snout into the dirt,
skittering grit onto my feet.

Chitter chitter the tusks. The peccary and I breathe together.
Yogic deep. Heavy. Dilated breaths. One finger out,
I reach, touch, bend one stiff bristle.
The javelina thruffs my scanty cricket's leg, knocks me back,
scrapes the skin of me and flees.

The Scrape of the Barrel of
My Father's Revolver on My Teeth

The scorpion disguised as a boy, disguised as a stepbrother,
went for the .44 hanging in the holster on the cowboy's

bedpost, held it to my head, and told me, *if he dies...*
Every beat in my chest went squishy *wait. wait. don't.*

The boy looked at me and seethed. I looked at him and waited.
He pressed the gun into my cheekbone. He did not shake.

Or worry overmuch. My head softened. Swam. *He's going to
kill me.* The bag of Der Wienerschnitzel went cold on the

table. He shook the barrel at my face, looked for the safety—
it wasn't latched but he didn't know that. The bleat of the

goats in the pens outside moved away, and the empty
farmhouse hung between us. My heart squished on. He

practiced in the desert on Coors cans with a shotgun and
trussed hay bales on Sundays. I did earthquake drills

in school. The phone rang beside us, and I thought I was dead.
He answered. The gun pressed into my face, smearing my lips

into a crooked gape that mirrored how I felt. He held out the
phone at me and with another shove at the barrel pushed

my lips aside and scraped my teeth. A gun on your teeth
sounds like the grind of spur on gravel. No, it sounds like a

gun on teeth. He walked casually, swinging the revolver,
strolling from the room unviolently, unconcerned.

He's going to shoot me, I cried to my mother in Santa Ana,
hours away by any means. She called the police who came *to*

keep the children company until some adults could return
to the scene. The cowboy was a deputy sheriff.

When the cowboy and the stepmother arrived home
to a cruiser in the drive he hissed, *that nosy woman*

should be drug out behind the barn
and shot.

My Father Warned Me of Javelina

Javelina had settled in the desert beyond the farmhouse
with some piglets, and the cowboy warned me,
They will gut you with sword tusks. Which is true.

They eat the prickly pear, smell rank, thick with musk, worse
than dogs, *if you hear the chitter chitter*
        of their tusks, then
        you better run.

He warned of rattlesnakes. And scorpions. Taught me
that the desert into which I was born was both beautiful
and deadly. He taught me respect for nature. Sorry, no.

That's not true. He never warned me
of anything. Except boys of a certain shade. But those
boys never harmed me once. Unlike him.

Cowboy Gives the Boy a Four-Wheeler ATV

and me, a girl, a three-wheeler. Because *he can handle it.*
Cowboy sold my horse at auction. *Won't need that damn*

animal. Because now there are ATVs. Tells us, *Tear it up.*
He coaches us to burn donuts and run through the sage bushes,

teaches us how to race and kick over the barrel cactuses,
how to chase jackrabbits, quail, and nesting birds.

But something holds me back. It doesn't
feel right to rev the engine, to watch lizards scatter in fear.

What is resilience if not the red flag of a failed system,
if not the cultural black eye behind her sunglasses,

if not the last look in a broken mirror?
And me parked under the mesquite, dreaming of birds and

lovely things, of lonely things like the flowers atop
the saguaro, always out of reach.

The fruit of the saguaro is unbearably high,
only vulnerable to birds. The cowboy is angry at me

for *being lazy instead of getting out there, having fun.*
I crawled through the pits at the base

of a saguaro with three fruit in my hands, traded for mice from
the traps, nailed up a door made of *I will not be like you*

to the hole, and locked myself in. Sheathed, I stood up inside,
stretched out my arms, *Roadrunner how do I talk to spiders,*

collect bones, taste the minerals in the water, make a home?
I did not ask how to kill a rattlesnake. Maybe because I didn't

trust myself to know who was and who wasn't. I condensed
inside the saguaro because the rain did, because

the wren did. Once there, I made a nest. Arms stretched
into green sleeves, spiny mask of saguaro to look through,

filled with the hope of water. A Sonoran duster. I wore the
cactus like I was finally safe, licked salt from my lip,

licked the sweet inside walls of the saguaro. The wren
in the penthouse flushed in a twist of fussy wings. On dollar-

store sandals, in an Olive Oyl T-shirt, I shuffled through scrub,
trekking toward the bay. It's an eighty-seven-hour
walk to Santa Ana where lives Mama.

And children shouldn't have to be resilient.

the mother and
the mountain
A FABLE

Remember where you came from, where you're going,
and why you created this mess you got yourself into
in the first place.
—RICHARD BACH

I

My mother was a bajada. That is, an alluvial fan that settled at the base of a mountain. Mama and the cowboy she made me with met at the Colonialist bar owned by her father, the dairy farmer who *was* a mountain. Bajadas fall from mountains and gather from plains, are left behind when streams pass through. This bajada, in particular, had slid down through Colorado, having been born of the dairy farmer and a stern woman, a mother's mother, who was a thalweg, which is a line. My mother arrived half-alive and twentysomething in a herald of dried clay, milk, and grit in Arizona. She stopped in Yuma to work with her father because he and she needed to remember love, having fallen away from each other. They needed to catch the breath of each other, to remember the scent of the tops of their heads. He was a mountain, her father. And he needed to show her the way to the sea as mountains do. Her being in Yuma to answer that call—halfway between her birth and the sea—was when she met the cowboy in her father's bar.

She was tending bar, the cowboy was stirring up dust. Colonialist was a box with windows up too high to see out of, or into. A lair. A box of men with a swamp cooler at one end near the ceiling, whirring enough to drown out soft talkers. Though those are not the kind of men who gathered at the Colonialist. There was a pool table in the center, and stools forever. The main point of Yuma, of the Colonialist, was the BAR with a rocking R above the mirror. Rows of bottles, most picked up by the farmer cum entrepreneur himself in Mexico on his twice-weekly summit over the sand line the white men call a border when it suits them, were the primary decorations. Mama was a short woman with a steady eye and in charge of everywhere she stood, whether her father was there or not.

The cowboy had gathered all of the cowboy things of a cowboy life because he'd come to Arizona by way of North Dakota. A hat—creamy and made of woven shantung straw, the *"bad boy types" wear black, these days. and the John Wayne types wear white,* her father told her, like men come color coded. This one also came with leather boots that had scuffed toes he polished every week on Sundays, though he didn't go to church, claiming "real men" didn't go to church (or eat quiche). He owned three pairs of Wranglers, one of them pressed and hung so he had a nice pair for evenings out. He kept a few women here and there, and a kid he'd left in Nebraska. Both of which he treated like belongings. On the boots were spurs that often went unnoticed unless or until they were used on a mule or, more often, on a horse he was breaking.

The bajada of a woman wore heels, not boots, and her hair added three inches to the top of her, making her five-foot-seven at the bar and five-foot-four in the morning. *Here's your beer,* were her first words to the cowboy. And his were, *You don't know it yet, but you're going to marry me.* Others had won and lost this game. This cowboy wasn't her first rodeo. But he was the most confident. He thought he was a mountain. And after weeks of her resistance and his persistence, she began to believe him. He reminded her of James Garner, of feeling rebellious, of the way her mother twice burned her blue jeans, but her father praised her fistfights. She measured herself against him. He filled up doorframes with his shoulders. Hooked his thumbs in pockets where his fingers could rest nearer the pistol. He reminded her of Westerns. Of Louis L'Amour, of coffee that has to settle before drinking, of boots on a porch, a belt on the bedpost. Of biscuits and cast iron, of freezing enough elk to see you through the hard winter Yuma will never have.

It was 1962. Against the man she was sure was a mountain, she looked small as lupine. She decided that her mother had been right. Mountains are easy to recognize. And maybe she shouldn't wear blue jeans. Bajada went back to wearing the scorched bra she'd lit but never finished burning. They married at the courthouse in California and posed for a snapshot in downtown Yuma.

Being the alluvial feet of mountains, bajadas lie close to largeness before they slide into the sea and therefore believe they belong with mountains. Having come from them, they look for mountains in everything they touch. *That's one?* No, don't be absurd. *Oh but he is definitely a mountain.* Again, no. He is a cowboy. *Listen, I swear, he's a mountain.* They stubbornly insist. But even as they look for mountains, bajadas are sliding toward the sea. The floor of the ocean holds all of their sorcery, their ancestry, the bones of the women from whom they come, the ashes, teeth, and salt, so they must go, and for some, this makes them melancholic, wilted and foregone, a little lost in the moment, like the future is waiting at the other end of the line, as when her father, far from bent and aged, developed colon cancer, and they knew immediately the road they were on.

Mama and the cowboy picked pecans. Wore daylight in the sunniest place on Earth. Made love to the sound of the scream of the kestrel, broke each other and horses, rode the air currents on their backs. Is it any wonder their daughter howls at the moon? They wrote dirges to seeds and played them on their skin. Soon, she forgot that she was a bajada and started to believe she was a cowboy's wife, picking pecans, loading sheep, cooking for rodeo night, excepting that by their tenth year together, she had borne and lost six children—four were lost in the midstages and two, whom she buried, were born the dead quiet color of the Colorado, and it broke her spirit. After the last one, she still slept in the shack but spent her days in the deepest shadows of the pecan grove, took off her bra, and started to tell the truth of the man she'd married. The way he drank, what he did after work—and who he had an eye for whether he drank or not. She sat, bare woe—

> in the desert scrub
> eyeing the moon
> trying to remember.

Every seed of every woman has lived in the womb of every woman before her. In this way, all of the women who will ever live, have ever lived, already exist and exist still. On and on, to the back of the cave. Mama moaned to the women of her line of her misery with this man. And that was when I was conceived. The doctors warned her not to try anymore because she would lose another, almost certainly. But these two wanted to be tied together, wanted their complicated natures to have a home outside their bodies. Which boggles, given what transpired.

II

Before birthing a scree-laden bajada, the mother's mother, the thalweg, was a streambed, a descendant of glaciers. She came from glaciers who moved slowly across the land, from glaciers who broke things, horses, and people. This woman was a streambed who *came from* glaciers, not a glacier herself, and although not a glacier herself, streams that are cut by glaciers continue to cut the land themselves in a generational tragedy for which the Indigenous pay the price. These people, we people, continue to break things as we move, always believing we should be somewhere, have a right to be anywhere we choose, always looking to get there, or get back to where we came from. This is why streams move in snaking motions, looking left, right, looking for a place to belong. Left, right, around the corner, next to those reeds? They jump and tumble and hunt for a home, often wishing that the glacier had never trekked across the land, never pushed them to be so far away, rushing headlong into the sea. And this woman was a streambed who settled into the deep lines of living in one place, snuggled up close to a mountain, then called him home like he was the point of everything. This was her man.

Now, that man was a genuine mountain. He and his thalweg came out of the Oklahoma dust bowl and made a life in Colorado. She wrote her family story in patchwork and darned socks; she loved in cast-iron skillet gravy, and having first survived the Depression, scratched life out of a dairy farm gladly. If her man milked cows and then went to Mexico "for entertainment," she wouldn't complain because he never lied about it. Honesty was his call sign.

When he was arrested for being drunk and disorderly, she fetched her mountain from a Mexico jail where they beat him near to death, and then she never mentioned it again. She made stern seem like a comfort. She didn't blame the arresting officers— thought about thanking them, but just took her mountain home and let it go. That mountain once walked across three states, across three Western states, and back, to bring home a donkey they needed for plowing. So for all of that Mexico business, she knew that her mountain had, that all mountains have, two sides. And this one was often cloudy at the top.

Mama came to the streambed and the mountain in the midst of a storm, squalling like she was already mad. She slid over the streambed, fell from the mountain, and ran toward the sea but never reached back—and for her mama this was the dam that stopped the heart of the stream. But before they broke each other, first she was born and first my mama grew. She grew and grew, mentally, emotionally but she never *grew* much, was always short and thin—although somehow, she took up all of the space in the room. Grandma forbade the alluvial, gathering nature of her bajada. There would be no blue jeans, motorcycles, swearing, or boys. And it turned out that these were Mama's favorite things in all the world.

Grandma was a rocky streambed unsuitable for the bare feet of a bajada who could not swim. They struggled with one another, wavered in and out of a love they rarely got to focus.

Every day, the lilacs woke the bajada in the morning light, with purple air rolling through the open window, forgotten ajar from sneaking back inside. Mama quickly looked nothing like the little girl who'd once found refuge in the cave of lilac branches. Well, yes she did. But her twelve-year-old eyes saw twenty-two in the mirror and she went barhopping, passing nights with cowboys (pedophiles) twice her age, but she was still a girl unless you asked her.

The burn on her leg from the pipe on the Harley of some cowboy streaked red rivers from ankle to thigh with puffy, pussed, and weeping skin. She wore her longest skirt and white knee-high socks to keep the growing infection from her mother. She was just a girl. No matter what they (or she) said. I know she was a girl from raising my own, but at twelve she'd have let me date men too, if I'd asked, so you know she wasn't a hypocrite. The girl, and later the woman too, just hated rules, would walk through the OUT door without noticing the rebelliousness of having done so. Came to be called rule breaker—and worse. She went looking for a life.

In the annals of 1954 men were right by default. And she stood alone like she'd won the lottery stones when they slung words through her confidence against cheeks turned down, stained her with slut, whore, for picking fights and loving her body. She rubbed berries on her lips. And put up a tent in the yard, a fort. The walls she made from the scraps of the skirts she'd been wearing every time she was called a whore. They told her she was loud, so she laughed louder.

On summer nights under the open sky she brushed the backs of her fingers along her jaw, closed her eyes, and said, *I love you*, in a whisper, imagining tenderness. Remember her this way. This is her photograph, and let history bury me as long as you know *I was hers*. But she and her mother never found solid ground.

Though not for lack of trying. *Child, your storms break on me. The way you rage if I push at you. In the workaday life of the dairy, I forget— but you make me so angry. Acting like compliance is a cuss word. Broke your brother's nose with a shoe polish bottle. Who does that? And for being a boy, stomping your sandcastle like boys do. My mountain on your side, defending you always. And he says, "She's defending herself like she ought. That girl never broke someone that didn't deserve a breaking." How can I compete with him for your love? If you aren't gutting yourself, spraying blood five feet in the air through a cut artery, and near dying, costing me seven years off my life, and costing us the year's earnings in hospital bills, then you're drowning and damn near dying when we fish you out of the water gone blue. You're a first-rate troublemaker in the way a girl shouldn't be. And stubborn. Mean to boot. I was loyal and protective. What else should I have been?*

Of course, bajadas shed scree on their way to the ocean. But do those stones cry out from the edges? No, they walk on, head held high, and get on with it. Except when it comes to leaving their mountain. Where begins the mountain and where ends the land? And the bajada of her couldn't shake off her mother fast enough. *When will you let go, Mother? And how do I?*

The women never made peace. There were always mountains in Mama's eyes. At birth she leaped into her father over her mother, because she saw a mountain in him. But when Grandpa died, Mama was there for her mother out of all of them. And maybe that's some kind of peace. There is an appealing honesty to the labor that becomes of a life despite what is lost. There is only drowning in the honesty of the passage of a mother who knew her daughter. Even if that daughter misjudged her mother.

And the stream outside the window under which she died spoke up to deaf ears; my mother never really knew her mother, but they both knew their daughters. And years from then, when I held her as she, too, took the long way home, she would look west from the window and say nothing of her mother. But instead, it was mountains even then, as she said to me, *It's okay. Don't be sad for me. I've loved a lot of men.*

There is a patchwork tent in my mother's scree, in her scramble, in the rocks, her sediment, her slough. She keeps her memories in a scorched tent with crumbling ashen edges, walls, and no roof. There, she is Loud. She grows a girl inside. She keeps the tent close, west of the pecan keeper's shack. Here with an open sky— she never meant to close out the sky—she hid from the cowboy behind billowing walls that puff and move as if the tent were breathing, and she birthed a girl under a Libra sun and Capricorn moon. It was 12:29 a.m. Twelve also being the number of hours she labored for her child before the Twilight Birth, and twenty-nine, although she wouldn't know it for years, twenty-nine being the number of years I would have a bajada to call my mother.

The cries of birthing screams and wails did not carry or echo across the desert, because there were none. The sun had gone for the night, so the stars peered over the walls of the tent. The night birds listened for a baby's cry and the mama slept while her body labored. She woke to find a redheaded infant had crawled from her and lay between her feet, looking for the door. The cowboy was in the nearest bar.

Quietly, before anyone could hear them and come to see the baby, the relieved mother touched water from a jar of Pacific Ocean to

the baby girl's breastbone, tucked a lilac seed under her tongue, and nodded once. She was satisfied. She'd made something tangible of this time of her life. This time with the cowboy. She spread out. Her hips widened, her breasts dipped lower, and her belly softened into a pillow. Before taking the child to the shack, to lay her under the window in the desert air, my mother sat with me,
bare woe—

        in the desert scrub
        behind patchwork billows
        eyeing the moon
        through the absent roof
        trying to remember
        why she'd ever loved him.

III

The woman awoke. She opened her eyes. In the tent, she picked up her redheaded child and walked to the picker's shack to introduce her to the cowboy. *Shithead,* she often called her child in jest. They laid her in a bassinet under the window, notes of dust and desert from the open window to sing the desert into her.

Outside, a shaded respite from the desert for the child, for the women of the grove, the tent stood through desert monsoons, and cowboy rage, for women. In it, the mother kept the things she wanted her daughter to have, boxes and boxes of books, including her thoroughly marked copy of *Illusions,* and photographs, suitcases full of photographs, full of people the child wouldn't be able to name once her mother died, taking with her the names of the women who had preceded her and unintentionally stranding the child. There were black-and-whites of trees with women, women on farms, with mules and men, with guns and in bars, bootlegger women, southern women, and desert women, Oklahoma and Colorado and Arkansas and Virginia, and back, and back, women, Old Country Irish, Scottish, and Welsh women with aproned skirts. Women who didn't smile for photographs. *This is Emmaline, Ollie and Dottie, Daisy, and America.* This child came from women.

In the tent, though it sat in the Sonoran, there were casual veils of a fog at rest hanging from the tentpoles. The sleepy feeling of a morning mist. There were flashes of what might be— mavens, moving around corners, dashing capuchin daredevils, a chandelier. Broken stilts leaned in the corner next to a rolled-up poster of Ireland, which sounded like a seashell when pressed to the ear. While her mother worked the pecan grove, the girl spent a lot of time alone, slipped inside the tent, and there noticed that the tent contained more than she could see from the outside. There were lively waterfalls and stagnant pools, rocking horse— there were waste and fortune, pork chop bones, and shotgun shells cast on a nightstand.

The breeze billowed the fabric walls, shaking loose the sounds of a life spent running from the cowboy's temper *go, run, get out; he's angry that I took too long in the store; didn't get the window of the truck closed before the rain; spoke to his friend. Go, use the kitchen window, go.* There was smeared blood lost in the red of the walls looking like shadows—and just for the girl there were exasperated sighs that her mother trapped in vials in a row, on a wooden shelf, behind layers of dust, under corks made of *No, don't touch the good things I've saved for you.* There is lean and retreat in those vials, *careful don't fall,* and *here hold this,* with *would you listen for once,* and *what's wrong with you?* There are shelves of plates, silver, a dress with a clock for a zipper pull, a cat, and the smell of her mother's hair. There are piano scales and a jar of seeds, the pillow from her bed and a vase of lilacs. And there is her mother. *Swallow this.* And into the girl's mouth she placed the seed of a lilac. *This is a tent made by every woman who ever—ever ever. With doors to every woman whoever you might possibly become.*

The cowboy's charming nature rusted when exposed to the weather of marriage. He spent days roping, riding bulls, and nights in the bars and basements fist/cock/dog fighting. He was angry. Had always been, said some. Not one day particularly any more than another. He was angry. Had been since the long walk at war as a machine gunner started to come out of him. His wife let it roll from him, let Inchon spill all over her like she could help carry it. He'd brought it home, drank the blood of it in communion. If she let it come, maybe she could find the bottom of the ditch of it. She knew. No, she was told. She wasn't supposed to make anything else of it, not supposed to see nature or nurture in the man in the hate he wore in the cloak of his stare. Doctors told her to allow it and let roll. The preacher told her it was *her place to love him, support him, be obedient. Know that it's not his fault.* It wasn't her fault when he raged at her. When he said, *Antagonism is you, woman.* Let his fury flow and hang on to the sides of the ditch, *it's too slick, too steep, I can't climb out.* And of course he knew the woman was a bajada and had never learned to swim.

War is an irrigation scheme. Washing into the fields and out over the crops of families. Sloshing the topsoil. War is the irrigation of the fields that were once the Sonoran. And irrigation salinates the desert as war salinates life. The cowboy was a flood of war in the picker's shack, kicked skids over in the lunge for attention, something, anything to salve the wound. Red tally-marks ran sticky through her fingers from her lips after his nights out. The floor dissolved under them, but she wouldn't cry. The first night, the first drop of her body to gild the floor of the picker's shack in red accusation clotted into the memory of the women she'd come from and spun into her eye where it became her last girl, a red fleck beside the iris, a seed, a reason to go. And a reason to stay. A kestrel's scream of a girl. They named her *shithead*, and bajada stayed with a fraying temperate smile. A tissue paper boat to sled the dunes. She was fragile until she wasn't. Because she thought she was just a woman. She's a woman until she remembers she's a mother. And loudly unbecoming. How can the foot of a mountain be otherwise?

IV

Her dog attacked him once. The last time. And the cowboy reloaded. It was a German shepherd she'd raised. Once, but it was more than once, he reminded her with the back of his hand that she should be like his mother—the woman who spent the paychecks he sent back from his post on everything other than the college savings account for which it had been intended— asphyxiating woman who told her grandchild to never call again since she was born outside of a sanctified Catholic marriage. My mother should be like her? Should, should—a list of them came at her from every corner. Her own mother, the cowboy, the preacher who visited the farms. The workmen. She should make different cornbread—his mother never used honey in hers. She beat him at games in the pool hall, flirted. The foot of a mountain, she was Loud, smoked long brown More menthol cigarettes, drank gin and tonics, and laughed to shake the windows—before she married the cowboy, men back then and maybe always were drawn to her, then climbed over her on the way somewhere else, just to have done so with ropes and knives to win a day against a trophy.

She had been behind the bar and knew and had tasted, sipped and licked at all of the life she could find, more than the cowboy cared to admit, and other men had won and lost her, yet many more still wanted to try. But the cowboy needed her to ease his way in life, and so she stayed but mixed into the paste of her lipstick was salt. There was never desperation in that woman.

In her there was a loving, palliative hand for her father, the only true mountain she ever knew, when the cancer came. From him, she saved for shithead the surfeit of wonder he handed down. From him, she saved for her daughter a turquoise ring he'd been given by an Indigenous friend, and from him she passed on the lie that her daughter could be anything. She sat fasting at his side for three weeks, massaged his spotted feet and dignified calves until her hands slept and she followed. She sat humming the hymns she didn't believe in because he believed in them. And there came in the sitting, her knowing—she was already sliding into the sea.

To her young daughter, she held out a pebble from the dregs of his grave and said, *Here look at the stone, remember the Earth he was, see the tree, see the way the leaves turn and offer you the light, this is how you breathe. Remember his honesty and sense of justice. Swallow this. This is the taste of safety.* And into her mouth she placed a lilac seed, *it's smooth and sweet,* and the pebble, *but often hard to get down. Like you, he would walk ten miles to return a dime that wasn't his. Like you, he loved me and saw worth in me. Like you, I could not save him. Like you to me, I could not save him. Okay? You can't save me.* She had a laugh so loud that it embarrassed her daughter even at this age, and here, she laughed at her own maudlin bathos before sending the child away to play in the grove. There is a woman's paycheck in the creases of her forehead, in the lines of the feet of my mother, feet that began turning west long before she left.

V

Do not. Not with her in my arms. Don't you hurt her. But cowboys have fast hands that blur, ranching hands that grab sheep and rabbits for slaughter, hands that hang onto manes, horns, and turn away muzzles, hands that milk, castrate, hands that scrape skin into leather, hands that butcher, fillet, make fire, hands that rope, and hogtie, hands that rein. Hands that come on suddenly. Hands that blur. Hands that grab. She fell more than that he hit her. The doorframe broke first blood. She hit a door. Those? Those are only halls of doors. Doors happen to women everywhere.

The drips from her mouth pooled in her cupped hand, opposite the one holding shithead, who was silent, watching her mother, as they sat on the floor. A cigarette smoldered a hole in the linoleum, and for a moment, my mother burned the house to the ground. But instead she would scry the caught red puddle in her palm, a mix of blood and spit, and see horizons, see that she was a bajada, and if looked on from a height, she was inches from the sea. And suddenly, in a moment her mother must have heard from beyond the grave, she could also see that cowboys aren't mountains.

The next time a drop of blood fell from her fingers for asking *why didn't you come home last night?* the drop flew in slow motion while they watched. It whirled around the cockeyed brass chandelier in the dining nook in the two-room shack where the pecan trees waved through the cracks between the boards but the windows were sturdy. The drop flew and wound a ribbon in the air between them. The blood knocked a vase to the floor, slammed a cabinet door, and stained the cowboy at his sternal notch with a smear.

As if there could be a sunrise, as if the day ever began again, she tied a string to the clouds that don't exist in a Yuma sky, blew out a smoke of *I love him*, until it became *I hate that man*, which fell in drifts of piles of ash around the trees, took the little shit by the hand, and walked from the shack while he slept.

She rolled up her tent, made the child a pecan pie for the road, and resolved her foot to the gas pedal of a tangerine Pinto. With her daughter bouncing on the seat in size-two shoes, they tore off the rearview mirror and rolled west. They rolled through scrub, over gravel and pit mines, over rattlesnakes. Straight through the desert, they rolled. Sprawled flat as divorce papers, she rolled.

Shoulders thump, thumping across the Sonoran, one after the other. Arms waving in windmills, they rolled. a kestrel screamed from the telephone wires. The child thrilled at the kestrel calling, *killi killi killi killi killi*. They rolled. They rolled over roads, pricker burrs, and bottle caps, they rolled over three men and a scrap of tin roof, over smog, over pipe smokers, cactus, and tusks. Over crying, over vows, over grackle. A mourning dove rode in her hair for three hours until they stopped for the night and set up the tent outside Joshua Tree. There, she took aim with her tongue and shot the mourning dove dead of shame. With the light clear and direct as pointed fingers, the woman lay topless in the sand in the sun, her hair a disaster of goodbye. Though the coyote, rattlesnake, and scorpion race against the night as a rule, this day all three came to settle in the sand around her.

She told her daughter, *You will have to go back sometimes. I can't keep you from him.* And ran her fingers through the hair of a coyote. *Maybe you get your wild-ass hair from the coyote,* she mused. The child cried. She didn't ever want to go back. The rattlesnake shook a warning rattle. She refused to quiet, and bargained. Then begged, but there would be no moving her mother on this point. Her mother looked the scorpion in the eye and said, *you are no mountain,* then threw it by the stinger, back into the desert. *Stay here. Don't follow me or I will shoot you.*

They rolled until Arizona covered their ears, pierced them with prickers, tattooed them with the juice of a beetle, stuck and slid into their mouths and eyes. They rolled over Los Angeles. The bajada slid toward the sea. They rolled until they came to the edge of the water of the Pacific and there stopped. There laid. There breathed. As the sound of the crash of the waves, the sound of the water washing the sand, the sound of the popping of seaweed drying in the sun, the click of barnacles opening and closing on rocks touched them, Arizona cracked and fell away, freeing their ears. They could again hear each other. When she finally heard the ocean clearly, she waited and waited longer, more and still more. She held herself back, waiting for the water to reach her crusted eyes, to grab her and take her to the ocean's breast and wash away everything that had happened in the last years.

Her daughter sat on the dune, throwing sand, pulling seaweed over her head like wigs, chewing on a stalk of dunegrass. When the waves came close, Mama rolled away to make it last, make the tide chase her, to feel wanted. She could hear the sound absolve the sand. Bull kelp fronds made her pillow, cool and tangy. Breathing in waves, her eyes came clean at last, and she could see. The salt washed onto and away from her lips. And she was able to speak. And I wish I could say she came to see she didn't need a mountain. Never had. But maybe it's enough that I learned it by watching her. Together we sat. A woman who could not swim and a child who blamed the desert for making her feel unsafe, we sat, bare woe—

> on the ocean's dune
> remembering every woman
> eyeing the moon
> and as I looked at my mother
> the ocean rolled out of her.

after

The courage that my mother had
Went with her, and is with her still;
—EDNA ST. VINCENT MILLAY

There is no quarrel possible in this silence
—ADRIENNE RICH

Even Heroes Have to Die

Nineteen? Yes, the nineteenth will do.

—MY MOTHER'S LAST WORDS,
    spoken as she was dreaming, and she did,
    indeed, die on the nineteenth of December.

And so mine did. Holding my hand
as the sun came up. She was a tempest,
an alluvial slope who looked west and went.
She did not wait or even wait for me

but rushed out for the ocean, which can't be right
because she couldn't swim, but looking west she breathed
until she did not and smiled a little into the last exhale.
I held onto her with my left hand, and the clammy

hands of my own daughters with my right.
An eruption of tear-stained seeds sprang from my cracked
open chest and soaked my mother's hair.
Why not leave in the night; why wait for morning?

Was it that she was dreaming?
But the woman who rose at sunrise every day of her life
did so then. And I cried until I dried out
drank the sea   and cried again.

From twenty-nine to thirty-nine I cried.
And from thirty-nine
to forty-five I cried. And forty-five on.
I washed some of her ashes into the sea,

tasted some of their salt on my tongue in the wind,
and cried because that's the doing of it.
I worked and raised my children and fell in love
with a yellow lab crying still.

I ordered in restaurants and cried, walked
crying   drove   crying
and I danced. And every time I thought of her, I cried.
But mothers are always moving, always saying goodbye.

Walking away as they leave you in school is practice for
taking their harvest of stones and stories with them
when they go, stretching out, out, pulled in every sense—
elongating the people who love them. They're

a walking helicopter game, when it goes faster and faster—
and their whole body reaches out to hold on and let go
at the same time. They're the pull of being the last one left
in the car, of being the last one breathing in a hospital room

such that the entire queue steps up one spot. And we are pulled
into our place in line by the impossible stretch of holding
on to the hands of our children and the hands of our mothers
while watching the latter, die.

I Lied to My Mother as She Lay Dying

i lied
                        when i said i'd be alright
how many years

        did you carry me?

i lied when i said   i wouldn't fall apart
i lied   when i said   i wouldn't fall apart
i lied when i said i wouldn't iiiiiii.   fall apart
i lied when i said i wouldn't   fall   at your feet
fallow   i wouldn't follow   you   said i wouldn't

                        i'm apart falling
            i lied
i lied when
                        wouldn't
said
                        i fall fell   I'm apart
iii said   lies

Under the Only Tree for Miles

When I finally got out, I scalded the desert. Razed it in my mind. Refused it from my life. Barred my feet of it. In my heart, I burned it to the sand, then burned the sand to make glass. I turned on it. The whole of the desert and everything, everyone, in it. No exceptions. I was running away at 180 knots, headed west and north and out to sea to get away from the desert, but I wasn't always and didn't forever. When I returned as an adult, crying still and growing dry inside, I plowed my shame into the sand and laid the blame at the feet of the scorpions, the prickly pear, the mesquite. Dryness longs for the desert and retreats there to mourn the ocean. Sand is strewn over centuries carried by feet worn into hooves. The sand, once an ocean floor, calls the dryness to itself while stretching out for the ocean's hand. My feet land on Saltillo tiles, the kind I would roller-skate across with a rhythmic bump bump bump. Red floors, red roads, red clay on the roof, by the river-blue sky unbroken, blue tile courtyards with fountains in front of adobe houses of river clay coupling river to home. The niceties of the modern desert life married to the a/c and divorced from the desert gloss the pentimento of the Sonoran's antagonism. Where went the desert of my youth? The scrub and prickers, the sweat and rattlesnakes? I'm on my knees with remember. This is where I learn who I am? Maybe this is where I learn who she was—the kestrel calls out in echoing cries *killi killi killi killi killi* but I ignore them. The coyote's chitter in the den is gone. Bitch to kit, I don't care. I wished the Sonoran silent. Under the only tree for miles. Miles that run the lines of river, border, state, and country—switchback of sand. I sit and burn it all. Cattle skulls top the posts shot through with rusted barbed wire the color of ancient leather, the scent of 1978. I dig for traces of my mother and cry. Scratch out holes looking for the sorcery of a woman who thought Mesa Verde was the most beautiful place on

Earth because the cowboy was nicest when they lived there. Heat blossoms as the red of the thermometer inches toward the porch roof. Drinking detail, I'm set on slow, sipping whiskey, spending moments one at a time, a miser. The pecan pie from the diner tastes like it came wrapped in a box. Thirst hangs off me where water tastes nimble but evaporates before I can be quenched. The day has scaly raking claws, thruffs me agitated with tusks for minute hands, scrapes me hot and bleeding. I cry. Sun ribbons paint my thighs under the only tree for miles. The cowboy dies somewhere. In a home with not one person left truly loving him. It's not justice. It just is. I come from women. I sit in the desert and scrape it away, set up an hour in the night that leaves me hungry for 360-degree eyes. I sit, bare woe—under stars thick as driveway gravel—and howl. I howl and cry *killi killi killi killi killi*. I howl. I howl. And that night, nesting as I am in the Sonoran, I realize it was never the desert that I hated, nor the desert that hated me.

Unruly

artistic, a little wild, this child
is in need of a comb. mama was always
tucking my *wild-ass* hair behind my ears.
i'm not exactly the kind of daughter who
has any idea what's best. i'm everything
i shouldn't be. just by being what i am. i
returned to the ocean, looked at the sea,
felt the silt of my mother in the waves.
looking back at her life, i perched
on a dune. in my hand, plucked from
the edge of her life, i held a lilac's first
spring bloom.
with great care,

        i sat,

               in the ocean's calling wind
               eyeing the carcass of a moon
               above the water
               which housed the orca
               trying to remember

where she ended and i began. was i dead?
my *wild-ass* hair whipping back   and forth
unruly   i heard on the waves and remembered
vividly the way she would tuck it behind my ear.
bare woe howled from me as the tide rose
to meet me where i sat. *killi killi killi*
killi killi, I called—and the sand
washed from my feet
came out of my hair   my eyes.   from the lilac
i gathered a seed and swallowed it with a mouthful
of seawater.   the ocean rolled out of me.

NOTES

Part opener "The Sunniest Place on Earth" quotes: Susan Griffin from *Woman and Nature*, and Combahee River Collective from *The Combahee River Collective Statement: Black Feminist Organizing in the Seventies and Eighties*.

"The Sunniest Place on Earth" (poem): The Yuma Territorial Prison (YTP) housed inmates on the banks of the Colorado from 1876 to 1909. In 1910 Yuma High School moved in to the prison and was housed there until 1914. The high school teams are still known as "The Criminals" and their store is called "The Cell Block." Around this time, 1880–1900, some sisters from Sacred Heart also operated an "Indian School" at Fort Yuma.

"The Confluence": Yuma is home to the Yuma Proving Grounds, one of the largest military installations in the world. KOFA (pronounced like sofa) was the name of the King of Arizona mine, which operated from 1897 to 1939, and the acronym is now used in multiple places in Yuma, including a wilderness area.

"The Crime Might Just Be the Law": No Más Muertes, also called No More Deaths, is an organization founded in 2004 in Arizona whose mission is to stop the deaths of migrants along the southern border. Among other things, this important organization aids volunteers who trek into the desert to leave food, water, and support supplies. No Más Muertes accepts donations of both funds and supplies at nomoredeaths.org.

Part opener "Estivate So You Don't Die" quotes: The Chicks, song title, "Not Ready to Make Nice" which has frequently felt like an anthem for me, and Zora Neale Hurston from *Their Eyes Were Watching God*.

"The Mother and the Mountain": A "Twilight Birth" was a form of birthing first used in the twentieth century in which drugs (morphine and scopolamine) given to the laboring mother caused her to birth in a drowsy state and to have no recollection of the birth.

Epigraph to "The Mother and the Mountain" comes from Richard Bach's book *Illusions*, Mama's favorite.

Part opener "After": Edna St. Vincent Millay, from "The Courage That My Mother Had" and Adrienne Rich from her poem "Harpers Ferry."

Special thanks to Cory for permission to use "Even Heroes Have to Die" as a title, which she said so casually after hearing this poem, like she's not at all a poet, proving that she is, actually, whether she believes it or not.

Printed in the United States
by Baker & Taylor Publisher Services